GREENER AT HOME

Over 200 Simple, Practical Tips on

Greening Your Environment

Copyright © 2012 Humus Amoris

All rights reserved. No part of this book may be used or reproduced in any manner whatsoever without the written permission of the publisher.

Printed in the United States of America. For information, or if you want to purchase in bulk at discount rates, please visit **www.humusamoris.com**

Library and Archives Canada Cataloguing in Publication

Tourville, Michel, 1973-
     Greener at home: Over 200 simple, practical tips on greening your environment / Michel Tourville.

Includes bibliographical references and index.

ISBN 978-0-9865456-1-0

     1. House & Home Sustainable living 2. House & Home Remodeling – Renovation- Energy Efficient 3.Nature: Environmental Conservation

II. Title: Over two hundred simple, practical tips on greening your environment

The paper used to produce this book is coming from responsibly managed forests under the regulatory standards and social responsibility goals established by SFI®, FSC®, or PEFC™.

Three percent of the sales proceeds from this book go to projects on greening our environment.

Table of Contents

Over 200 Simple, Practical Tips on Greening Your Environment 1
Table of Contents 3
Preface 4
Let's Put a Stop to This Madness... 9
How toxic are you?... 10
Greening Your Home 15
Cutting Down on Your Consumption 19
Cutting Down On Your Waste 33
Celebrate Earth Day 36
Making Your Home Energy Efficient 40
Laundry Management... 51
Tap Into Alternative Sources of Energy 54
Making Every Drop Count.. 59
Smart Appliances and Construction Material.................................... 71
Construction: Going Green from the Ground Up 80
Food for Thought 87
Care for Your Domestic Animals.. 104
Holidays and Celebrations 108
Outdoors 112
Garden a Little 118
Summing Up 124
Index 125
Additional Resources.. 128
Web-Based Resources 133

Preface

Humus Amoris, founded in 2008, has a very clear mandate: to reduce people's ecological footprint.. Humus Amoris is there to jettison us out of our cozy, comfortable life, and awaken us into doing something completely unforeseen, different and exciting.

Having difficulty making changes to our lifestyle, is not unusual. When we become aware of our wasteful ways, we are often clueless about how to make ecologically responsible decisions.
Although over the past few years we've been flooded with a glut of information on "greening our

> **How Can You Make the Best Use of This Book?**
>
> Very simple.
> The book is not loaded up with highbrow theory, but it provides practical ideas that you can apply at home straightaway and that will help you create an environment awareness in your children.

environment," having information overload is almost akin to having no information at all!

After a point, it becomes hard to understand how everything fits into the big picture. Most people, when asked about environment conservation issues, would be aware of only one or two things they could do to make a difference, but that would pretty much be the extent of it. We want to go beyond that kind of tokenism. We want to make a substantial difference through our own efforts.

After doing research for our first book, we came to the conclusion that it was hard to find resources where we could get comprehensive information quickly and all in one place. There were loads of resources available, but none of the kind we were looking for. Most were short compilations of the "top 10" lists that were quick reads and that did not leave us any richer in information. Many provided too little or too much explanation laced with elaborate technical details that only eco-savvy people could understand or use. Nothing for ordinary people to apply in their daily lives.

That's when the penny dropped. We came to the conclusion that most people just want to leave a cleaner planet for future generations. We are not militant environmentalists, championing some vague, lofty principles. We just see common sense in taking earth-friendly action.

Indeed, we belong to the category of people who don't necessarily want the whole encyclopaedia thrown at them—we just want to know what simple things we can do to bring about a change. In addition, we would like to know the impact of our actions, so that we can develop our own plan and tweak it where necessary.

From our experience, we've come to realize that generally people don't want to change how they are living too much. They don't want to commit to drastic measures, but just want to take a few tentative baby steps, directly observe the impact of their action and keep moving down the line in a positive way.

So, while preparing for our first book on small organizations, we began to gather information about real people making a real impact on their surroundings. The idea is to consolidate all the information into one resource for easy access.

Although we live in the Internet age, we feel that a book (paper or electronic) is the right format for this project. Websites by definition demand a lot of navigation, but nothing can beat the user-friendliness of a book that you can earmark and pick up where you leave off. For those who prefer the Web, and in order to make this book accessible to as many people as possible, we do have an online version at www.humusamoris.com that you can log on to, anytime.

As with our first book, our intent once again is not to have a tome packed with lots of verbiage. We've seen enough books—sometimes with 300 pages or more, that could easily have been reduced to one tenth the volume, without compromising any information at all!

The main objective of this book is to gently infuse you with ideas—not to bombard or overwhelm. At the end of the day, all we want is to provide you with practical, sensible ideas.

Why not include fun information on transportation, sports, and activities outside your home? Why just concentrate on eco-friendly activities inside your home?

The answer is fairly simple. Since, our core concept is about values and changing peoples'

NIMBY (not in my backyard) mindset, we thought the best place to start would be on the home front, since that's where our own education begins, and that's where our children learn from us.

As you flip through the pages of this book, you'll find many hands-on, practical ideas that can, without exception, be put into practice by each and every member of the family. Many ideas can be immediately applied, while some may become more relevant or useful later on. Nothing is exclusive to time and place, making all concepts truly relevant in all contexts. One simple example is reducing water consumption through low flow shower heads. Doing this will still be a good thing, even five years from now.

If you want to know more about us, log on to http://www.humusamoris.com. Aside from promoting eco-friendly events, activities, tips and products through our website, Humus Amoris also donates three percent of our sales proceeds to greening our environment.

We hope you enjoy reading this book as much as we enjoyed putting it together!

Let's Put a Stop to This Madness

Quick, answer these questions:

- How many days in the week do you travel by public transport?

- Do you recycle all your books and newspapers?

- Do you switch off your car while waiting at a traffic light?

- How frequently do you eat junk food?

Don't be embarrassed by your answers; we're all in this together. The majority of us are living a non-sustainable life that would need at least four to five planets like Earth to give us all the resources we need!

If we carried this scenario to its fruition, the result could be an *Avatar*-like situation, where some might feel the need to invade another planet and rob their resources, just to fill a personal need!

Think about what will happen when all the natural resources on this Earth are consumed and there is no way to replenish them. Think about all those heaps of e-waste at landfill sites that are non biodegradable.

Think about what kind of a planet you are leaving behind for your children to inherit.

Does this mindless waste not rattle your consciousness?

Fact is that you, me and everybody else can make a difference. Incorporate little changes into your lifestyle and you can make a BIG difference to the environment that you live in. You certainly don't have to take a big leap and involve the whole community. That can come at a later stage. First, let's take small baby steps within our own families.

How toxic are you?

Ever thought about how potentially toxic your life is? Log on to http://wwf.panda.org/how_you_can_help/live_green/footprint_calculator/ to find out the pollution impact of your footprint on Earth.

After you have discovered how toxic your life is, we will take you on a guided tour of your house—the living room, kitchen, bathroom, attic, etc.,—to find out what the issues are in each location and how you can adjust your surroundings.

A detailed look into these spaces will follow later.

There are two areas in which you can make a change to your lifestyle:

1. in your wasteful consumption

2. in "greening" your life. That means increasing your consumption of green foods, wearing green clothes, using green technology, following green practices, etc.

This book will discuss the environmental impacts of both these steps.

The first thing you can do is log on to www.naturalstep.org. This website is run by an organization called The Natural Step, and is founded by a Swedish cancer specialist, Karl-Henrik Robèrt. After consulting colleagues and scientists, he came up with a four-pronged model for maintaining a healthier life on Earth. Dubbed The Natural Step Framework, the model became so popular, that it's now being adopted by trans-national companies such as IKEA and McDonald's. Briefly, here are the four principles of this model:

1. In a sustainable society, nature is not subject to systematically increasing concentrations of substances extracted from the earth's crust.

2. In a sustainable society, nature is not subject to systematically increasing concentrations of substances produced by society.

3. In a sustainable society, nature is not subject to systematically increasing degradation by physical means.

4. People are not subject to conditions that systematically undermine their capacity to meet their needs.

As a consumer, when you buy things without bothering to find out the item's ecological impact, you run the risk of breaking the following principles:

Example	Principle Violated
Paper made out of virgin fiber	3
Products made out of non-recyclable ingredients	2
Spraying insecticide on your lawn	2
Buying metal products made of virgin metals	1

However, you support these principles when you...

Buy coffee marked with "fair trade" label	2 and 3
Order organic food	2 and 3
Improve the insulation of your home	1 and 3

This last one is pretty interesting in application. If you live in a coal-rich area that makes its electricity principally from coal, you subscribe to Principle 1. However, if the electricity is generated through water (hydroelectricity), you are subscribing to Principle 3, since dams significantly affect an area's original landscape.

I bet you never knew this!

There are several such ideas that you are going to discover in this book. So, stay tuned.

Greening Your Home

You can be part of this process of change wherever you are. There are various websites where you can go to get started, but we recommend the Greenhouse Gas Protocol website at www.ghgprotocol.org.

Assess your current state

Although most of the ideas in this book can be applied without any particular sequence, the one place you need to start is to first assess your baseline. You need to know where you stand today and where to go tomorrow. To identify your baseline, you need to cover all types of waste sources: water, energy and general waste (recycled or not).

Let's first start with water consumption.

Do you have any idea how many gallons of water your family consumes in any given month?

No idea?

Most of us don't have the foggiest idea how much water we consume. I presume that your house may already be equipped with a water meter against which you pay a monthly water bill. But do you bother to read your bill?

If you don't, I would suggest you begin to do so for at least a few months. At the end of this exercise, you'll be surprised with what you discover.

If you do not have a meter, you may have to work a little harder. Begin by listing all the ways that you consume water during an average week. Showers, watering the plants, food preparation—you name it. Once the list is complete, evaluate each activity's water consumption and start doing the number-crunching. You may not be a math whiz, but believe me, the more effort you put into this exercise, the better the end results will be.

As a second step, you need to assess your energy consumption. If you are hooked up to the grid and don't have a secondary source of energy, just calculate your annual consumption from the electricity bill you get monthly. If you have a second source such as gas, add your gas consumption to the sum. Do the same for wood usage. This way, you'll begin to see the full picture. Next, measure your consumption in dollar terms, as each unit comes as gallons of gas or as Kilowatts (KW) if the source is electricity.

Third, measure your waste. This may be the toughest step in this exercise as you don't actually get billed for waste (aside from your municipal tax bill). But, what we suggest (as in the above exercises) is a systematic approach. Count how many trash bags you put out on the street every week. Better still, if you have a scale at home, weigh your garbage.

Do the same if you have a recycling bin and compost pile. Although recycling is considered a good idea, it's still a form of garbage and in the hierarchy of waste, the best waste is the waste that does not exist at all—however impossible that may sound. Also, not everything that is put in the recycling bin gets recycled, but that's a different story altogether, certainly one that is beyond the scope of this book! Instead, what you CAN do is gather as much information as possible from the recycling centers close to your home. Armed with this baseline, you will then be able to measure the changes you make at home. After you are done with all the steps mentioned here, you may not want to repeat the exercises each month, but even if you do it every three, six, nine or twelve months, you'll definitely be on your way to making good progress.

Cutting Down on Your Consumption

You may have heard the dictum "more is better." This may be true in most cases, but it is not true when it comes to conservation. Before making a purchase, ask yourself if you really need to have this particular product right now, or if it can wait. If the answer is that it can wait, then it's wise to postpone the purchase. Chances are that you will never buy the item—never. Your immediate need has passed or you've moved on to something else.

There could be another way out of getting rid of excess waste. Get in touch with your local authority or church and spread the information around. Inquire at your office if someone is interested in secondhand stuff. Or better still, organize a garage sale or a swap/barter day where neighbors and friends can exchange their functioning appliances. There are agencies like Freecycle.com where you can do this online.

Here are a few other tips that you can follow at home...

Give a second life to products

If you are building an outdoor shed for your lawnmower and patio furniture, why not put in a used door or a used window? When you are in the process of buying furniture or lamps, why not look for antiques or rummage through yard sales? You would be surprised to know that you can land something really eye-catching!

"Just in case" purchases

Ever bought something just in case, only to realize that you have three of the same products lying around unused at home? If you are unsure about whether or not you have the item at home, don't go in for that kind of a buy.

Bargain

Avoid all kind of bargain hunts. Buy what you need, not what happens to be the cheapest stuff in the marketplace. That way you're only going to be collecting more junk.

Envelopes

The obvious thing to do when you get bills or letters at work is to recycle the envelopes once opened. But you can also give a second life to them by using them for your "to do" list. If you fold the envelopes, they will be the perfect size to slip into your back pocket. They also have better rigidity than a common sheet of paper, so you can easily check things off as you complete them.

Cash register receipts

The obvious thing to do when you empty your pockets or purse and find cash register receipts is to recycle them. But you can also give a second life to them by using them as draft paper for grocery lists or to-do-lists. Keep a stack close to the phone in case you need to jot down a phone number.

Reduce toilet water consumption

If you don't have one of those new toilets that uses less water, drop a brick or a bottle filled with water into the water tank. This object will take care of the volume, thereby reducing the amount of water used with every flush.

Repair your shoes

When your shoes start to give out, consider repairing them instead of throwing them away. Leather shoes are the best for repairs, but even running shoes can be fixed and made to last for another three or six months. Visit a local shoemaker and you'd be surprised to discover what he/she can do to keep your shoes going.

Phone book

First make sure you recycle the one you have. Next, get on the phone and call your phone company to inform them that you do not need another directory because you've discovered a more eco-sensitive way of looking up phone numbers—the online directory!

Cleaning products

Did you know that almost every common stain can be removed with vinegar and or baking soda? So why buy 35 different products to do the same job?

Cut down on napkin use

...even if the napkins are made of paper or cloth. Let's not forget that the cotton industry leaves its own footprint on the environment. The frequency of napkin use should dictate your choice. In restaurants, where napkins are washed and discarded frequently because of color fading, it might be better to go for paper napkins; but at home, where the use is less frequent, cloth napkins would be a clear winner.

> **You Too Can Contribute**
> WWF shares a vision with other organizations on the future of paper, and in this action uses materials from the joint project. Log on to www.shrinkpaper.org to find out more.

Even when buying cloth napkins, select linen napkins since they absorb less water. To wash linen napkins, always use cold water and phosphate-free soap, and hang dry them.

There are a million little ways that you can cut your general consumption inside your home.

This, of course, is just the beginning.

Consuming Right

According to capitalist thinking, the only good thing a consumer can do is buy, buy and buy.

Today, there can be nothing more detrimental for our planet than such a philosophy.

Here are some good "green" options you have when you go out to buy…

> **Green hangers**
> Did you know that roughly 77 million wire hangers end up in landfills each year? Or that a wire hanger takes over 100 years to break down at the dump site? This is something that gave three friends – Christian Ferrante, Ash Singham and Josh Cohen – the inspiration to come up with wireless hangers crafted from recycled paper.
> Source: http://www.abc.net.au/insidebusiness/content/2007/s22750

Dishwasher products

Pick soap without phosphates. Most dishwashers are as effective if you fill the soap dispenser only half way so don't fill it to the top. Use vinegar as a rinse. Vinegar is just as effective, if not more so, as any other commercial product, and is far less expensive.

Recycled packaging

If you have to choose between two similar products, choose the one that respects the environment the most, even down to the packaging.

Ecological logs

Ecological logs are made from various wood residue and coffee grounds that are compacted very densely. They do not attract insects, they burn longer and they generate more heat.

Toilet paper and tissues

Buy those made with 100% recycled material. Increasingly, these products are being made without whitening agents such as chlorine.

Also, Greenpeace does an audit of all the popular toilet paper brands and gives a thumbs up to those that aren't eliminating old forests in the process.

The audit is based on three criteria. The brand under examination should

- use 100% recycled content

- consist of at least 50% post-consumer recycled content

- be bleached without toxic chlorine content

http://www.greenpeace.org/usa/en/campaigns/forests/tissue-guide/

Dry cleaning

The traditional dry cleaning process used to use solvents that were toxic to the environment. Today, many of these companies are much more aware of what they use. As the consumer, first, try NOT to buy clothes that require dry cleaning, and second, know that certain dry cleaners use only carbon dioxide as a cleaning agent, making this process far less harmful.

Eat at green restaurants

Patronize restaurants that strictly follow green business practices such as those that use toilets with low water consumption or those that list organic food on their menu. Some also do composting and recycle bottles and plastics.

Office supplies

Buy adhesive notes made out of recycled paper and 30% post-consumer content. If possible, replace your markers with a solvent base, and ink with chalk, wax pens or colored pencils.

Always use binders more than once. Every year, see which ones are still good and which ones need a little repair, and then try to find binders made with recycled materials. Furthermore, buy only scissors made with recycled stainless steel in the blades and 30% post-consumer plastic.

Fair trade flowers

These flowers contain fewer pesticides and make for wonderful gifts for someone you really care about.

Look for the EPA certification

The Environment Protection Agency (EPA) certifies companies that conform to green practices.

Dryer balls

If you must use a dryer, consider adding dryer balls to cut drying time and to avoid using fabric softeners.

Lighters

Choose matches over lighters. Lighters are made of plastic, contain fuel, and are usually thrown into the garbage. Also, when buying matches, select cardboard ones as they are made of recycled paper.

Magazine subscriptions

Subscribe to your favorite magazine instead of buying it at your local newsstand. You'll save money and it will be delivered right to your doorstep. Did you know that the magazines not sold on the stands often end up in the trash?

Rent DVDs

Even a committed movie buff doesn't watch his favorite movie more than two or three times. Renting makes more sense.

Movies at home

Better than going out to watch movies, download them at home. Not only will you save on gas but you'll also be sure to see the movie you really want to watch!

Purchase refurbished electronics

Refurbished does not necessarily mean cheap or secondhand. Often, for whatever reason, these products are returned to the stores within a few days of purchase. Sometimes, products used as demonstrators, discontinued products, or those with small defects end up in a warehouses where you can buy them at attractive discounts (sometimes as much as 40%)! Sometimes they even carry original warranties. Check out www.dyscern.com and www.refurbdepot.com for a selection of such refurbished electronics.

Throw away bio-degradable plates

If you must use disposable plates or utensils for a particular event—birthday, picnic, etc., buy corn-based products that are biodegradable.

Trash bags

Even if they are not the perfect size, reuse your leftover paper and plastic bags instead of buying new bags. You will save money and put out less plastic into the environment.

You can buy oxo-biodegradable bags that break down more quickly when exposed to water and sun. They may be made with petroleum based products which is not good, but on the plus side, since they break down more quickly, their materials are absorbed by the landfill more efficiently than other bags. Hence, they take up less space over time.

Corn-based bags are easily available today. They may be a bit more expensive and not very strong, but the latter can be easily taken care of by not overloading them.

So, every time you are about to buy or consume something, ask yourself if there is another option that leaves a smaller footprint.

If there is, you know what choice you need to make.

Cutting Down On Your Waste

Recycle your electronics

Get paid to recycle your old gadgets. There are services like www.buymytronics.com, www.myboneyard.com and www.greenphone.com that will keep them out of landfills. Simply call them to collect your item and then wait for your check. Handset manufacturer Nokia, for instance, has recently placed such boxes in several countries. Your cell phone vendor may also offer a buy-back package. Check with him. Finally, it's possible that your local community sponsors electronic waste disposal and recycling. Check this out from the government pages in your phone directory.

Recycle your clothes

Clothing companies such as Patagonia (www.patagonia.com) and Mountain Equipment Coop (www.mec.ca) in Canada take back used clothing and weave the recycled fibers into new clothes.

Recycle your refrigerator

If you have to dispose of an old refrigerator, check if the manufacturer will take it back. In Europe, it's the retailer's responsibility to take back your old appliance.

Recycle those batteries

If you were to keep a count, you'd be surprised at the number of batteries you use, especially if you have children. Use an old ice cream or yogurt container to hold all the used batteries and take the container to the local hardware store. Sometimes, they'll recycle the batteries, or a local electronic store may offer a handy place to drop off unwanted batteries.

> **Just a Minute**
> Always recycle your paper, glass, plastics and other waste. Consult your local directory or phone service to find out about an agency that also offers a collection service.

Donate and recycle DVDs

If you decide to do some spring cleaning and need to overhaul your DVD rack, take it over to a DVD recycling center. Google will help you find the recycling center closest to you.

Free "at your door" advertising

If your mailbox gets stuffed with unsolicited sales material, write to those companies to stop sending you this type of mail. You'll be glad to know that these companies offer the same rebates online. So why on earth do you need their printed brochures? Call them and ask them not to deliver their fliers to your house.

Celebrate Earth Day

Mark that date down in your calendar as a red letter day where everyone in the family can see it: April 22nd.

Throw a party for your friends, your children's friends or friends' friends and organize a memorable event around Earth Day. If possible, make it more significant than birthdays, Mother's Day, Father's Day, etc., although those are also important. Make some noise. People need to celebrate Earth Day. This could be a good opportunity to take stock of the past year's environmental balance sheet, examine the actions you took, or missed taking, appreciate all that's green and clean and beautiful on this planet and congratulate yourself on your successful input to the green cause. Think about it—why not organize a land clean up?

Get your neighbors and friends to bring some trash bags and have them clean the local park or the community center. It would take just about an hour and leave you feeling so good about the clean look of your park. What's more, it will send a powerful message to your children who, after all, learn by imitation. Be an important role model to them. After the clean up, you can have some fun with games, contests (the winner could be the person who brings the biggest bag) and refreshments. Just make sure you don't leave any trash behind.

Give clothes a second life

If you have some clothes for discarding, organize swap deals. You could also donate the clothing to the poor.

Service as a gift

Instead of buying a gift for a new neighbor, or thanking them for something, offer to mow their lawn, rake their leaves, shovel their entranceway or take care of their house if they are going away. Share power tools and other appliances. They'll appreciate your help. This will also build a stronger bond between the two of you. And who knows, maybe they'll offer you the help next time!

Recycle

Did you know that a person can easily reduce his waste by 75% by recycling paper, glass, aluminum, etc.? Think about the impact on the landfills, and think about how the world would look if we did not need to produce new things.

There are three important elements to recycling:

Firstly, you need to draw up a list of your household products that can be recycled and assign a storage space for them. Go the extra mile in looking for stuff that could not have ended up anywhere except on the recycling route. Pick up things left on the street in front of your house or at the park when taking a walk. This will send the right message to others.

Some retailers have a clothing recycling program. Check out Patagonia (www.patagonia.com); they use plastic bottles in their fleece.

The second step is not just to put stuff that you don't need any more out on the street, but taking it to your local recycling center to be turned into pots and pans, mattresses, etc.

Third, and final, have the courage the patronize the recycling industry by buying products made out of recycled materials such as paper, clothing or plastic products.

Making Your Home Energy Efficient

If we keep burning coal, gas and oil, the scientists' consensus is that by the latter part of the century, the planet's temperature will have risen five degrees Fahrenheit to a temperature higher than we've seen for 50 million years.

Remember, energy efficiency is cost efficiency, too. Therefore, before doing anything about upgrading heating systems or insulation, you need to first tackle air leaks. To do a simple test, light a candle on a breezy day, and take a walk through your house looking for places where the smoke drifts. Sealing these gaps is usually easy. On the outside of the house, silicone usually does the trick. If you can put some insulation inside as well, you will have taken care of most of the heat loss.

Old houses usually lose a lot of heat through the windows. Remember how your grandpa used to seal windows in the winter with plastic barriers? This simple measure can cut heat loss by as much as 25–50%.

Insulate pipes

Insulate your hot water pipes with foam. This will decrease heat loss from your water heater to sinks and showers.

Keep curtains drawn

In the summer, closing curtains keeps the sun from heating the house and in the winter this provides additional insulation.

Minimum heat in the garage

North Americans heat their houses more than necessary, and this applies to garage heating as well. What a waste! Instead, keep the garage temperature above the freezing level simply by improving the insulation. For starters, make sure that the joints are tight. When building a house, some people don't bother to insulate their garage wall in order to save some money. Better assess your needs again. One simple thing you can do is turn the heat completely off when the temperature gets warmer. In general, keep the heat lower than you would think necessary.

Reduce heat in scarcely used rooms

Often, we try to have a comfortable temperature wherever we are. But does it make sense to heat the basement when you spend less than five minutes a day there? What about the unused rooms upstairs? You can easily preset these areas to one or four degrees cooler, and if you need to spend more time in them for whatever reason, turn the heat up a little; it should take only a few minutes to be comfortable again. What if you just need to get something quickly? Resist the temptation to turn the heat up, even if you are a little uncomfortable. Remember that for the next 23 hours or so, that room is going to be warm for no one!

Right heating

Use programmable thermostats for your rooms without connecting them to your central heating system. The advantage is that you can then reduce the temperature of individual rooms. Also, when you are at work and the kids are at school, reduce your home's temperature by one or two degrees. There is no need to keep the place warm when nobody is there. You will save 5-10% on your energy consumption on a yearly basis. Programmable thermostats are better because their precision is higher than the old models. You also end up consuming less energy by keeping the temperature consistent.

A/C in the summer

If you live in cooler climates, air conditioning is not a must-have. Recall the time when people did not have air conditioning and they still survived. Instead, use the conventional, equally effective methods of cooling, such as taking a shower before going to bed, making sure the house stays cool during the day by drawing all the curtains, and so on. Plus, if you have cold weather the rest of the year, why not enjoy a little bit of the heat that you've been waiting for the whole year?

Switch off the lights when they're not in use

Keep the lights on only in the room you are in, and switch them off when you leave the room. It's as simple as that. Teach your kids this habit especially in relation to places that are not often used, such as the attic, garage, etc.

Light tips

How often do you wipe the dust off light bulbs?

Never, you say?

That's bad because merely cleaning your bulbs will save you energy. If your wall color is pale, luminosity will be better and you can then comfortably turn off the surrounding lights.

Timer on lights

Keeping the patio light on when everyone inside the house is sleeping has no logical basis. If you really need the patio light, make sure the bulbs are eco-energetic and are on a timer.

Motion activated lighting

Use motion sensors to activate at least a few lights at home. These can be used outside on the patio, or inside to keep the low traffic areas well lit. Also, have a timer attached to the sensor so when there is no movement, it automatically gets turned off.

Replace your bulbs

Did you know that traditional bulbs convert just 5% of energy into light and 95% into heat? In contrast, the ratio for a compact fluorescent light (CFL) is that it converts 80% of the energy to light and 20% to heat, and the CFLs last far longer, too. But wait, don't rush to throw all your regular bulbs in one shot. Start replacing them gradually with CFLs. Although the CFLs function with gas, they can still be discarded at any approved recycling center, and their benefits far exceed the drawbacks. Make sure you put these bulbs in rooms where the light stays on for a good period of time, as turning them on and off reduces their life span. If you turn on a CFL light and need to leave the room for a short time, leave the light on.

Stop the water heater during your vacations

Why have you got your water heater on if you are NOT going to use it for a week or two?

Instant water heater

Instant water heaters now exist. Instead of keeping the water in a tank and keeping it hot even when the water is not being used, this instant heater is located close to the faucet and heats only when the hot water tap is turned on. Remember, however, that if you use a lot of water, this device is not very efficient since the pressure is less than it is coming from the conventional tank. Also, this device can be plugged into only one exit, so it is practical only for small apartments. As an alternative, just go for a few smaller tanks, instead of one huge overhead tank.

Timer during vacation for lights

If you absolutely want to keep burglars away while you are not home, instead of leaving lights on or the radio running, put your lights on a timer. You will save money and it will serve you better as potential burglars will notice that lights are going on and off. Clever, isn't it?

Use electricity at the right time

Try to cut down on your electricity consumption during peak hours, i.e., from 7:00AM to 9:00AM, and then again from 5:00PM to 7:00PM. Start your laundry or dishwasher at night, instead of at lunch hour. You may want to go bi-energy using heat with gas at those times and switch back to normal the rest of the day. This way, you'll give some respite to the common electricity grid.

"Energy Star" products

There was a time when just a handful of products such a washers and dryers, freezers, etc., carried an energy star logo. Now, this label covers over 35 categories of products. And more often, these products command a premium price because the technology on which they've been developed is a little more refined and expensive. However, before buying one such product, make sure you consider long-term costs during the life cycle of the product in terms of the energy and water consumption and maintenance costs.

Rechargeable batteries

The impact of using rechargeable batteries in the home can be huge. Think of all the homes in your city, region or country that consume batteries and how much we would save if we switched to rechargeable ones.

Ice pack in the refrigerator

Lots of energy gets used for heating during the winters. One way to reduce the amount of energy used is to use a cold source (like an ice pack) to keep the refrigerator cold and control the amount of heat getting into it each time the refrigerator door is opened. Use two ice packs in rotation, keeping one outdoors so that it freezes in the cold, and the other inside the refrigerator to maintain the cold temperature. Switch the ice packs daily to reduce the refrigerator's energy need to keep the temperature cold and steady .

Refrigerator maintenance

Place a sheet of paper between the refrigerator door and the opening, then shut the door. If you can take out the sheet of paper easily, it means the door is not properly sealed. Also, make sure the back of the appliance is dust free by cleaning it twice a year. Dust diminishes the heat flow, therefore reducing your appliance's effectiveness. If your refrigerator is more than 10 years old, replace it with a new as they are far more effective. Make sure your old refrigerator is disposed responsibly.

Heat loss from the oven

Every conventional oven has one of its grills open to allow heat to escape. When you are preparing dinner, you can use this grill to preheat water for pasta or heat up some vegetables.

Remote control power strip

Even when your electronics are switched off, they consume power. We now have several gadgets (computers, TV's, etc.) that are seldom switched off even during the night. So, here come power strips with a remote control device to help you easily turn off all electronics and completely shut down their power supply.

Unplug your TV

When you are not using your TV, unplug it. About 10% of your TV's energy is still used when it is turned off. Appliances like this are called vampire appliances as they suck idle energy all the time. The same thing applies to your VCR, DVD player, printer and coffee machines.

Now that you have reduced all the unnecessary energy consumption in your house, let's look at how you can buy renewable energy.

Laundry Management

The first thing you need to watch out for when doing laundry is the number of times clothes have been worn before ending up in the laundry pile. You might find that some of these clothes really don't need laundering, and this will help you cut down on the number of washes you do during the week. Next, try to buy concentrated phosphate-free detergent. These detergents will save on packaging and transportation, since less detergent will go farther in use. Know that phosphate damages natural ecosystems such as algal blooms in rivers and lakes.

The washer you use also makes a difference. Front loading washers can cut your water usage in half, depending on the age of your machine.

Wash in cold water

Make a habit of washing everything in cold water. Nowadays, with the quality of the soaps and washing machines, everything comes clean even with cold water. Try and see the results for yourself, first with towels and heavier items, and check the results. You'll save lots of energy, too.

Hang clothes to dry

This is a simple one. Not so long ago, our grandparents used to hang their clothing to dry. Now, we have the luxury of having drying machines and seem to have forgotten that clothes can still dry outside without electricity. In an ideal, futuristic eco-world, we might have solar dryers, but until then, why not hang your clothes out on sunny days? Another way out would be to select specific clothes for the dryer. For instance, maybe you don't mind a little wrinkled or stiff exercise outfit or shirt that you will need to iron anyway. By putting fewer clothes in the dryer, you will use less energy. People living in cooler climates can hang dry their clothes inside. This will actually improve the humidity in the house. Just be careful not to put the clothes in a small room without proper ventilation since the humidity can spoil your walls and/or window frames.

Dryer tip

When you have young kids, it seems like you are always having to wash clothes. It is a never-ending process. When using the dryer, however, make sure the filter is clean. An obstructed filter requires more energy to run. Moisture sensors are another way to cut the drying time as they stop your machine when they sense the clothes are dry. Plus, you are better off with full loads. Most dryers that stop when the clothes are dry work with a sensor that detects a certain temperature (not humidity). It usually doesn't get to the right temperature when there is too much humidity, but that heat makes the water in the clothes evaporate. With partial loads, you need almost as much energy as you would need with a full load to get the temperature hot enough so that the water will evaporate.

Tap Into Alternative Sources of Energy

Unbelievable, but true! Electric companies now offer a choice between using the main source (which unfortunately is still mainly coal or natural gas) or an alternative source such as wind power. You can, at the click of a mouse, choose the electric company that will buy the equivalent amount of your energy consumption from a renewable source. In some states these companies are very competitive, and if more people ask for it, they will become even more affordable. Also, if you measure the true cost of using coal, it may be cheaper to burn but it causes more pollution and therefore has a hidden cost attached!

Sell your own electricity

If a small river flows near your property, if you have plenty of sun, or if you have strong winds blowing in your area, you can invest in renewable energy and sell the excess energy to your electricity provider. This way, you're not just saving on your electricity bill, but you're also making some money in the process! If your source is intermittent, this method can offset the cost of using network energy when your own system is not generating enough. Solar and wind technology have advanced greatly in the past few years and are now more affordable than ever. If you don't want to invest too much at the beginning, start small by just getting enough to meet 25–40% of your total energy needs. This will reduce your investment and get you started. You can gradually increase your electrical capacity if you have plans to do so.

Solar power

The simplest way to define solar power is that it converts the excess energy provided by the sun into electrical energy for running home or office appliances. Most city buildings have flat roofs which are ideal for installing solar panels that won't be visible from the street. That in itself is positive, as these panels are usually hot. But afterwards, these panels are not used for anything else. To use the solar panels, place them either on the roof, on a post, or a little away (make sure you check municipal regulations as some regions have restrictions on the size and type of panels they allow). Check on Google and you'll find tons of information on how to install these panels, on the different products offered, their comparative prices and the savings associated with each. Notably, solar panels are easier to find and are more cost efficient these days than say five to six years ago.

Geothermal power

Geothermal energy is produced from the ground. It uses the steady temperature of the Earth to heat or cool your house. This system uses as little as half the amount of electricity that traditional systems use, with a typical life of more than 25 years. They are more expensive to install than other systems, but they are useful both in winters and in summers when the Earth's temperature is cooler than it is on its surface on a hot summer day. So when you do your calculation, make sure you factor in the cost of running the system the whole year round.

Wind power

Wind power is proven to be an efficient source of energy for our homes. Wind power is more often used in remote areas where a grid is not present. But, of course, a windy climate is required to make this work. Once you have checked if your area is zoned to allow wind turbines, take the time to pick the right spot for installation by measuring wind speed and frequency with the right instruments. Don't hesitate to seek the help of a wind analyst. Make sure you also do a proper evaluation of your energy needs at home before you invest in the right size turbine.

To help you make progress in your quest for energy efficiency, we've put together a tear sheet with tips so you can assess what steps you've already taken and where there is room to do more. Just mark off what appears practical and feasible for you. Once you've put a few of these ideas into place, return to the list every few months to mark off a few more.

Topic	Done	To do
Insulate pipes		
Keep curtains drawn		
Minimum heat in the garage		
Reduce heat in scarcely used rooms		
Right heating		
A/C in the summer		
Switch off the lights when they're not in use		
Light tips		
Timer on lights		
Motion activated lighting		
Replace your bulbs		
Stop the water heater during your vacations		
Instant water heater		
Timer during vacation for lights		
Use electricity at the right time		
"Energy Star" products		
Rechargeable batteries		
Ice pack in the refrigerator		
Refrigerator maintenance		
Heat loss from the oven		
Remote control power strip		
Unplug your TV		
Laundry Management		
Wash in cold water		
Hang clothes to dry		
Dryer tip		
Tap Into Alternative Sources of Energy		
Sell your own electricity		
Solar power		
Geothermal power		
Wind power		

Making Every Drop Count

Some people wait until the water temperature is exactly as they want before plugging up the drain. If this is you, remember that doing so wastes a lot of water and energy. Plug the drain as you start filling the bath and adjust the temperature as you go along. Once you fill the tub this way a few times, you'll instinctively learn how to set your faucets to your liking.

Bottled water

Avoid buying water bottles. Although they are generally recyclable, the sheer volume of these bottles out there makes the capacity for recycling all of them almost impossible. Also, transporting bottles is a cardinal sin. They travel by truck and come from far. Think of the energy used just to get them into your hands. If you need to leave the house and know you will need water, carry your personal bottle. For safety measures, make sure to clean the bottle regularly to eliminate bacteria. If you are unsure of the water quality in your home, use water filters. There are several trusted brands available on the market, but the best known brand is Brita. This company has even kicked off an online campaign called FilterForGood (http://www.filterforgood.com)!

Brushing your teeth

Although this one seems obvious, there are still people who keep the water running while they brush their teeth or shave. Use enough water just to wet your toothbrush at the beginning of the process and to rinse it in the end, and you will end up saving a lot of water. To rinse your mouth, use a glass, not your hand.

Cold water to drink

You like to drink cold water, and for that you wait a minute or two with the tap running to make sure you don't end up drinking water at room temperature. That's bad practice. Instead, keep a glass or bottle filled with water in the refrigerator and drink as much as you want.

Dishwasher management

Make sure your dishwasher is full and that plates, glasses and cutlery are placed as per the manufacturer's instructions. This will ensure most efficient use of detergent, water and energy. Use the economy cycle and remember that with most dishwashers, you can put up to 25% less soap than required and still get the desired results. On some models, it's also possible to do a final rinse with cold water. Opt for biodegradable, phosphate-free detergent in powder form as this takes less energy to ship (*powdered is lighter than liquid*).

Don't pre-rinse the plates since most dishwashers are powerful enough to clean the dishes without this. Just use a little bit of water and scrub. Full loads save up to 35% of the water if not rinsed, as compared to washing dishes by hand. Also, most dishwashers use hot air to dry the dishes, so when you see that the cycles is at dry, just leave open the door and let the dishes dry gradually. If you have a timer on your dishwasher, set it to start during the night when the energy demand is lowest, as most people are sleeping. You'll also reduce the energy need from the grid during peak day hours. If you don't have a timer, just start your dishwasher when you go to bed.

Maximize water use while washing dishes

Dip your dishes in a sink with the right amount of water and soap, and finish with a rinse of clean cold water from a second sink. Avoid washing dishes under running water which uses more water and soap than needed.

Commercial car washes

Instead of washing your car yourself, have it washed at a commercial car wash. It saves water because the jets they have are more precise and efficient. Also, most modern car washes recycle and filter the water used, more than once.

If you must wash the car yourself, use a sponge and bucket and rinse afterwards. Use a biodegradable soap, such as Simple Green's Car Wash. Don't try to clean the car with just plain water. It's also preferable to wash it on your lawn instead of in the driveway so that the toxic waste water can be absorbed and neutralize the soil instead of running into the city's sewer system.

Driveway

Are you one of those people who washes their driveway with water? Who must make it sparkling clean so not a speck of dust remains? Using a broom instead will give you the same results and will also help you get rid of the rocks, sand and dust particles.

Low flow showerheads

Merely changing your regular showerhead to a low flow one will reduce your water consumption in the shower by half. You can also try an aerator showerhead for a totally different (pleasant) sensation! These devices are easily installed and are very affordable.

Recuperate gray water

You can install a system that recuperates the gray water from your house's sinks and washing machine. It filters it so you can use it for plant watering or for flushing your toilets. Combined with rain water, it would be sufficient to take care of your entire water requirement for the toilets.

Responsible water consumption

Water is needed for a variety of things, whether for drinking, cleaning (clothes, dishes, cars, etc.), heating, garden work, toilets, etc. In all of these activities, make sure not to waste any water. Public water is treated, and therefore needs processing, chemicals, filtration, and so on. As a taxpayer, you pay for all this. Also, although the water that is returned to the environment is treated and adheres to certain regulations, it's not of the same quality as it was before, so it can potentially damage the sensitive bio-diversity downstream.

The table below gives an idea of the water consumed in various activities:

Table 1. Water used in normal home activities.

Area	Activity	# of times	Circumstances	Water Used	Total
BATHROOM	Toilet	4 flushes/ day	Conventional toilet	3.5 - 7.0 gal/flush	14-28 gal/day
			ULV toilet	1.6 gal/flush	6 gal/ day
	Shower	5 min. once/ day	Conventional showerhead	3-8 gal/minute	14-40 gal/day
			Low-flow showerhead	2.5 gal/minute	12 gal/day
	Bath	once/day	Full tub	30-45 gal	30-45 gal/day
			Tub 1/4 to 1/3 full	9-12 gal	9-12 gal
	Shaving	once/day	Open tap	5-10 gal	5-10 gal
			One full basin of water	1 gal	1 gal/day
	Brushing teeth	twice/day	Open tap	2-5 gal	4-10 gal/day
			One full basin of water	¼ to ½ gal	½ to 1 gal/day
	Hand washing	4 times/day	Open tap	2 gal	4 gal/day
			Soap and then rinse	¼ gal	1 gal/day
KITCHEN	Cooking	Washing produce once/day	Open tap	5-10 gal	5-10 gal/ day
			One full kitchen basin	1-2 gal	1-2 gal/day
	Dishwasher	once/day full load	Standard cycle	10-15 gal	10-15 gal/ day
			Short cycle	8-13 gal	8-13 gal/ day
	Dishwashing by hand	once/day	Open tap	30 gal	30 gal/day
			Full basin/wash and rinse	5 gal	5 gal/day
	Laundry	once every 3 days	Conventional top-loader	35-50 gal	70-100 gal/week
			Front-loader	18-20 gal	36-40 gal/week
MISC.	Car washing	twice/month	Hose w/shut-off nozzle	50 gal/wash	100 gal/month
			5 full, 2 gal. buckets	10 gal/wash	20 gal/month
LAWNCARE	Kentucky bluegrass	½" every third day	5000 sq. ft.	1,500 gal/watering	18,500 gal/month
	Turf-type tall fescue	½" twice/week	5000 sq. ft.	1,500 gal/watering	12,500 gal/month
	Buffalo grass	½" every 2 weeks	5000 sq. ft.	1,500 gal/watering	3,000 gal/month

Source: *Water Conservation in and around the Home, Colorado State University Extension*

Make a habit of reducing your shower time. Every minute you cut down can save up to five gallons of water. Over one year, this adds up to 2000 gallons of water per person!

Also, try not to flush the toilet every time it is used. At home, if you know someone else will go too, save a flush. Finally, when you wash fruits or vegetables, do so in a pan and not over running water. You'll save lots of water and use the rest for plants. So don't throw away anything for nothing.

Running water tap

If you have water leaking from one of your taps, fix it immediately, even if the leakage looks small. One drop doesn't seem big but it can add up to a large quantity over the course of 24 hours. In some areas of the world, a drop a second for a full day is more water than they have in total in one day. Here is a rough estimate of water loss from a leaking tap:

Estimated Facet Leakage Rates (# of drips)
60 drops/minute = 192 gallons/month
90 drops/minute = 210 gallons/month
120 drops/minute = 429 gallons/month

Source: Water Conservation in and around the Home, Colorado State University Extension

According to Colorado State University, merely checking and repairing faucet leaks can save up to 140 gallons of water per week!

Water leftover

When you come back from work with a little bit of water left in your water bottle, don't empty it in the kitchen sink. Use it to water plants inside or outside, or use it for your pets. Plants are not picky about water!

Toilets

About one fourth of the average home's water consumption goes out the toilet if the homes are not water efficient. New models use about half of the amount water (i.e., 1.6 vs. 3.6 gallons) on average. For one person, this will reduce annual water use from 27,300 gallons to 12,500 gallons. This saves capacity for the water system upstream and downstream. If you need to shop for a toilet, choose a two-flush system that saves up to 40% if you flush liquids (i.e., only about 0.9 gallons per flush). There are several manufacturers of these types of toilets, but don't be fooled, a more expensive toilet is not necessarily the best. With competition, prices are coming down. But if you are not ready to buy a two-flush toilet, you can still improve your water consumption by simply installing a newer model.

Rainwater collection

Place a water barrel where it can collect rain water from your house's roof. In most climates, there is enough rain so that your barrel can keep flower beds and small gardens well watered. If going back and forth with a watering can is not your cup of tea, you can place your barrel on an elevated platform or on a cement block and then plug in a hose for watering. You can find barrels modified to plug a hose on the market. Check the Web also for a Do-It-Yourself (DIY) system.

Water early in the morning

Lots of people have sprinkler systems for watering their lawns. If that is the case with you, make sure the watering is done early in the morning before the sun comes up and the temperature rises. Evening watering could be better than mid day, but even though absorption is good, the ground stays humid for longer and this could be an invitation to fungus growth! Also, make sure your sprinklers are spread out properly so they don't water your house instead of your lawn.

Shaving

There are still guys who fill the sink with water when they shave or let the tap run throughout the entire the process. Use enough water just to rinse your razor, maybe two or three seconds under the tap, for a total of seven to ten times maximum.

Water in the pool

Don't fill your pool more than eight inches from the top and you'll reduce water loss from splashes. Also, by making sure that you cover you pool when it's not in use; you'll reduce water loss by evaporation and the water will remain hotter by saving energy when heating your pool.

Smart Appliances and Construction Material

Front loading washers

If you need to shop for a washer, choose a front loading one. As mentioned before, these washers run on less electricity and water, and do less damage to your clothes. Their drying cycle is also more efficient.

Furniture selection

Go for furniture made with natural fabrics such as cotton and ramie. Avoid using chemically-treated products as they release gas that's toxic and can affect the indoor air quality of your house.

If you choose wooden pieces, try to find ones made with wood from FSC forests or reclaimed wood.

> **Think Local**
> Locally available material is always a sensible choice. Focus, instead, on newer ways of featuring or assembling them.

Another material to look for in furniture is bamboo. Bamboo is fast growing in popularity and can be used for multiple applications. Recycled plastic and metal is also finding increased use in the furniture industry. Another way to conserve forests and ease loads in landfills is to buy furniture second hand.

Smaller oven

If you are thinking of buying a new oven, ask yourself if you really need a conventional size. The smaller ones are better and have been used in Europe for ages. Try to recall when was the last time you used the whole oven space. Maybe you never did. So if these ovens are not available where you are, search for them on the Web and have the oven shipped to you directly.

Solar water heater

In areas where it's sunny enough, this is a good alternative to traditional electricity. Water heating is one of the main contributors to energy consumption at home, so if you have sufficient solar heated water for your own use, you need less from the electrical grid.

Ventilators

Instead of an air conditioner, install a ventilator. It consumes less energy (at least ten times less) and will get you through those hot summer days in comfort.

Construction materials

If you are planning on renovating your house, select materials processed from recycled products. The employees at your local hardware store will guide you in the right direction.

Bamboo flooring

Bamboo is one of those things that the ecological community does not agree upon. On the plus side, it grows very fast and therefore gets replenished faster than wood, but it comes from far-off places such as China and India, which for North Americans is the other end of the world. Does the benefit outweigh the environmental costs? If you are deciding between bamboo and another exotic type of wood, bamboo should be your choice.

> **Strong, steely and renewable bamboo**
> Bamboo has several advantages...
> - Bamboo floors cost half (Rs180-220 per sq. ft) of what hardwood costs. Laminate is cheaper, but not as durable. Bamboo is tough enough for even basketball courts!
> - Unlike wooden fixtures that rot over time, bamboo bath accessories last for decades, especially if pegged together by bamboo nails that don't rust.
> - Bamboo blinds, unlike fabric, can be sluiced down or rinsed in the shower.

Carpets

Rugs are treated with stain-proofing chemicals, mothproof pesticides and more. Wall-to-wall carpets can't be removed for a good and thorough wash, and so, pollutants can settle in places more deeply than an ordinary vacuum can reach. Dust mites are a common trigger for asthma. Since 1980, the number of children with asthma has doubled. Pesticides and herbicides sprayed on lawns, lead dust from your neighbor's renovation project. In fact, anything blown or tracked into your house can settle into your carpet for years.

If you must have carpets, do the following: first, clean your carpets regularly. When buying a carpet, select one made of 100% recycled material. This type of carpeting saves the resources and lessens the load on landfills. The Interface Company (www.interfaceglobal.com) is a leader in sustainability and has contributed to revolutionizing best practices in the industry that it operates in. The company embarked on this journey in 1994 and continues to innovate and improve an industry that only a few years ago was hardly pro-environment. And finally, when you buy new carpeting, have your old carpet taken back for recycling.

Ceramic tiles

Ceramic is very durable and the resources needed to produce it are not overexploited. More and more tiles are being made with recycled material (glass, clay, etc.), so try one of those.

Cork flooring

The insulation that cork provides is incredible! And now cork comes in a variety of colors. Just make sure the varnish is water-based. Cork is also good for sound proofing and is quite flexible, so it can be used for a variety of aesthetic finishes. Since cork is a natural insulator of both heat and sound and is soft enough to absorb the inevitable bumps of childhood, cork walls make perfect sense for a house with little children. Cork is harvested just once in a decade from the outer bark of oak trees that grow in arid regions in Portugal, Spain, Algeria and Morocco. Flooring is made from the scraps remaining after bottle corks are punched out.

Double-paned windows

Choose double-paned windows. The space between the two sheets of glass contains gas (argon) and in cooler climates the surface reflects the heat. During the summer months, the external sheet reflects the heat back to the outside. The drawback in this system is that the reflecting agent is not environment-friendly and is not easily recyclable, as it does not fuse easily with other types of glass.

Garbage disposal

Compost whatever you can, and throw very little into the garbage bin. You may not know that the water used for garbage disposal can disrupt the delicate water ecosystem. A good exercise for those willing to get your hands a little dirty is to go through your trash once and see if you can somehow reduce the volume. Can you recycle more? Are you throwing things away that were useless and that you should not have bought in the first place? If for nothing else, this exercise should be an eye opener.

100% recycled glass tiles

If you are thinking of buying new glass tiles, get 100% recycled glass tiles. The advantages are numerous. First, recycled glass tiles are made by melting post-consumer and post-industrial waste glass. Also, because they utilize materials considered waste, less glass gets lifted to the landfill. Finally, recycled glass tiles absorb less fossil fuel than new glass tiles.

Polyethylene lumber

This material is made from recycled plastic containers and is generally used to produce outdoor furniture in parks and for making benches, picnic tables, decks trash cans, etc. The beauty of the material is that the color does not fade over time, and therefore it does not need a fresh coat of paint every two years. It's also resistant to insects and humidity.

Stone tiles

Like ceramic tiles, stone tiles are very durable. However, do look at the origin of the stone. The best option is to buy local stone. Since the material is heavy, the environmental impact of lugging the stone across several miles can be serious.

Wood flooring origin

Local wood or secondhand flooring (have it re-milled) is the best option. Exotic woods like teak, rosewood or pine may look nice, but forest extraction and transportation aren't worth the aesthetics. If your floors are in relatively good condition, they can be re-polished and refinished with a low volatile organic compound (VOC) product such as Polyureseal BP made of AFM Safecoat.

Wood selection

The Forest Stewardship Council (FSC) certifies wood that has been harvested with sustainable methods. It not only considers the environmental impact but also considers if the workers and local businesses have been adequately compensated for the work.

Construction: Going Green from the Ground Up

If you've read Ayn Rand's *Fountainhead*, you might recall the stunning description of Heller House that cantilevered over the edge of a cliff—the first house designed by the idealistic young architect, Howard Roark.

The house, made of local material, followed the broad contours of the rocks that it stood on, "rising as it rose" on the lush hillock. It did not stick out as a sore thumb. Rather, this was a statement, to borrow Rand's words, of unquestionable integrity!

In the plot, Roark gets expelled from the Stanton Institute of Technology because he refuses to follow their outdated building dictums. And for the rest of his life, he struggles to get his ideas accepted, until finally, he stops struggling.

Thankfully, architects like Roark would have a better chance of surviving in today's world, where gradually, we are awakening to the utilitarian aspects of buildings, rather than the aesthetics. A house, by definition, shelters those inside. It can blend in with the other houses, being non-obtrusive and functional, or still shelter and protect the people, but extend that to preserve the environment as well.

If this is a vision you share, read this section and find out how to translate this vision into practical terms.

One way to make insulation more efficient and maintain indoor temperatures is to actually build your house in the ground. In winter, you will likely still require a heating system, but you will need less than what is required in a traditional house. That is because the temperature in the ground is hotter than it is higher up, and the heat stays trapped inside because of better insulation.

Green renovation

When renovating, try to reuse the material that you've removed. If you can't use it yourself, find a local recycling center. They often accept construction material. Also, even though the building your are renovating may be old, use this opportunity to put in better insulation, low water consumption toilets, etc.

Green roof

In urban areas, where the roofs are flat, why not put up a green roof? Not only does it help reduce global warming, but you can also grow vegetables and plants there. A roof garden is also good for rain water management.

Heating and Cooling

As mentioned before, pick the most energy efficient appliance with an energy star logo. Also, make sure you buy the right size system to fit your needs. Prioritize heating from hydroelectric power first, then gas as second. Once installed, make sure you follow the instructions for maintenance so you draw optimum value from your system. You may need to clean or change your system's elements once in a while.

Insulating windows and doors

Let's face it. The best insulation would be to have only walls and roofs—no windows or doors! That's what Eskimos do with their igloos. But since that's not possible, invest a wee-bit more into energy-efficient windows. Windows that open using levers are more effective in the long run because they seal better. Sliding windows can become loose and lose their insulation value.

Window insulation

Whether your house is located in a very cold or warm climate, ensure that your windows do not let in too much air. This is not just a problem with older buildings that are not well insulated, but also with newer ones where the insulation is not as effective as it should be. Fortunately, there are a variety of products available at the local hardware store that can correct this problem. To check if you have air infiltration, light a candle and bring it close to the window. If the flame is not steady, i.e., there seems to be a draft, then you'll need to insulate.

Location for your home

When you are selecting an ideal location for your new home, include natural green elements as part of your selection criteria:

- Is it close to work, school, or wherever you frequently have to commute to?

- Will you need to cut down a lot of trees to build your house?

- Is the area close to a bus or train station?

- Does the city or neighborhood have environmental policies in place?

- Is the air quality in the location you are considering healthy and clean? The EPA has an index that measures ozone over several places in the US.

- Is your town recycling the minimum (glass, metal and paper) or are they going beyond that and do they have recycling centers that process and reuse articles? Do they provide a composting program?

Paint type

Did you know that paint can be made from natural substances such as citrus plants, milk protein, or clay? Such paint products come free of preservatives and biocides. However, clay paints do have some downsides: They may carry a little odor, and the odor does last very long—sometimes as long as 40 years. They also have a porous finish that needs sealing with natural wax to protect it from stains and liquids. There are fewer color options in latex paints (approximately 100) and plasters come in powder form and require mixing with water.

As for milk-based paints (yes, you heard right!), they are 100% natural, have little or no odor and are highly durable (can last for centuries if applied correctly). The only disadvantage (if it can be called that) is that they come in powder form, so they need to be applied quickly once exposed to air and water (within 12 hours). They also need sealing with natural wax to protect from stains and liquids. Milk paints have the least color options (just 30-40) and are the most expensive of all eco-friendly paints!

If you must use synthetic paint, try to go for the ones made from recycled paint with low VOC labels. Check the data sheet and look for the VOC level. You should not buy anything higher than 150 grams per liter.

Paint quantity

Before setting out to buy paint, check if you have leftovers from previous projects. If you find that the paint is no longer good, take the opportunity to have it recycled. If you must buy new paint, buy only the amount you'll need to complete a project and buy recycled paint with low VOC, as mentioned above. If necessary, you can always get more paint later on. In some places, they may even take the unused can back. If that's not possible, store the paint safely or dispose of it according to your local municipal regulations. Donate unused paint to a charity organization. They'll be very grateful for a fresh coat of color!

Painting tip

When painting indoors, throw open all windows and use fans to get rid of the fumes. Pregnant women and people with allergies or asthma should not paint and should stay out of the area for at least 48 hours.

Smaller houses

Small is beautiful. Extra square footage not only costs more to maintain, it also requires increased energy consumption, more furniture, gadgets and gizmos. Make sure you build according to your family size and needs and renovate only when you need to.

Food for Thought

Pre-packaged lunches some parent give their children are a good example of not just "over-packaging" but also a testimony to the quality (staleness) of the food inside. Remember, you are what you eat. Take the time to prepare something nice. Your children's health is far more important than the ten minutes you save in buying pre-packaged food.

Buy organic

Organic farming not only ensures food that is pesticide-free, but it's also a statement of sustainable development. Respect the soil, the air and the people involved with these products. Organic food is now available in most supermarkets and is used in restaurants and cafeterias.

Switch to vegetarianism

You probably know that meat requires more "energy" to make it to your plate, requiring more square footage and resources for storage and maintenance. Okay, going 100% no meat is probably hard if you are used to having meat at every meal. But try reducing meat consumption to one meal a day. See how your family adapts,

> **Must You Turn Vegetarian?**
>
> Not necessarily, but several health experts, such as Dr. Michael Brown and Dr. Josef Goldstein, recommend a diet free of eggs and meat for a disease-free life. A study to this effect, carried in *The Journal of Clinical Pathology* (July 2001), found that veggies are heart healthy. The study's findings were:
>
> - Foods such as eggs, fowl, fish, meat, etc., contain little or no dietary fiber, so they can cause bowel problems such as constipation, piles, colon cancer, indigestion, ulcers, diverticulitis, etc.
> - The yolk of the egg contains 250 to 300 mgs of cholesterol, which can harden the arteries, causing strokes, gallstones, etc.
> - The albumin (egg white) contains a substance called "avidin," which in certain cases can cause leprosy, eczema, paralysis, skin cancer, etc. Prof. Egnerberg of Germany found that eggs produce 51.83% of phlegm (cough) and disturb the balance of some nutritive elements within the body.
> - All types of meats / eggs contain saturated fatty acids that can block blood vessels.
> - If eggs are not properly stored (i.e., refrigerated), they begin to decay inside the shell if left at 80C for more than 12 hours. This makes them highly susceptible to fungus and virus growth in developing countries that do not have proper storage and stocking facilities for poultry products.

and then try to decrease the quantity of meat

you buy every week. And if nothing works, just reduce the portion sizes served on the dining room table.

Beans

You may laugh, but you can actually substitute beans for meat. At least with respect to nutrition, if not taste. Beans (of all kinds) are loaded with protein. Put them in salads or slow cook them in soups in the winter. There are thousands of recipes to choose from on the Internet. You are sure to find a few

> **Think about it**
> Recent reports state that farm animals cause more greenhouse gas emissions than automobiles. Now, environmentalist groups have become increasingly aware of livestock farming's adverse effects on the environment. Runoff from large-scale livestock production destroys watersheds. And do not forget the ethical concerns about the barbaric conditions under which animals are raised and slaughtered for human use.

that your family will like. As with other tips, try to do a bean meal once a week to start, and try it with a different recipe each time for surprise and variety! (All children love surprises!)

Fish is always better

Fish does not contain the saturated fat that meat does, so it's better for your health. However, be careful what type of fish you buy. In an ideal world, we would all eat wild fish, but thanks to our wanton exploitation of the natural sea resource, these too have become endangered. The best choice is to buy cultivated organic fish. By doing so you do not contribute to a declining fish population and you support a sustainable means of producing fish.

Organic meat

Don't do a double-take. If you've done all that you can to turn to vegetarianism and have failed miserably, buy organic meat. It will cost a little more as raising animals organic style is less productive—as is anything mass produced. If you've already replaced some of your meat meal with vegetables, then you've already begun to save because vegetables cost far less than meat. One is clearly a tradeoff for the other.

Buy concentrated frozen juice instead of fresh

Both products offer similar nutritive value. Frozen juice takes up less space and therefore needs less fuel to move from point A to point B. You may not know it but today, the beverage industry is the biggest fuel and water consumer around.

Coffee machine filter

Make sure your coffee machine has a metal or plastic filter. This will save you from using paper filters every time the coffee machine needs to be started.

Organic beer

Again, you may not have thought about it, but the beer industry consumes huge amounts of water and energy, besides using grains such as cereals. And in order to produce the best quality of beer, big multinational companies grow humongous fields of cereal and use chemical pesticides to maintain it all.

Therefore, the next time you have this urge for a beer, look for the certified organic symbol. By buying organic beer, you support a farm system that uses fewer or no pesticides at all and synthetic fertilizer, which in turn enhances soil fertility, increases species diversity, conserves water and produces fewer greenhouse gases.

Convinced?

Second, as with any food product, local brews reduce fossil-fuel consumption and greenhouse gas emissions when shipping the barrels. Microbreweries have become popular over the last few decades, so support them, even if the local brewery may not yet be selling organic beer.

Third, draught beer is greener than bottled beer. Each keg under the bar counter saves hundreds of cans and bottles. In fact, if you do a life cycle assessment, draught beer leaves approximately 60% less of an environmental impact than bottled beer.

Finally, make sure you recycle your bottles, and if you can, buy brands with no paper on the bottle, as in every cycle the bottle goes through, the paper is removed and wasted.

Organic wine

We now have organic wines that are certified by the National Organic Program (NOP). These products contain 95% organic ingredients and no added sulfites. To be certified as a 100% organic wine, it must contain 100% organically produced ingredients and organically produced processing aids, not counting added water and salt. The permissible limit is a maximum 5% non-organically produced agricultural ingredients.

Shade grown coffee

We've heard about fair-trade coffee, but shade grown coffee is different. On traditional coffee plantations, everything is taken down in order to plant the coffee trees in the soil. What this does is create a monoculture that attracts certain insects and diseases that are then countered with pesticides and fertilizers. By keeping the original plantation trees intact and interspersing those with fruit trees, the soil and coffee trees become healthier. Besides that, bigger trees can host birds that can feed off insects, further reducing the need for chemicals.

Substitute milk from animals for milk from plants

You have the choice of soy, rice, or almond milk. You name it and you can have it. By choosing those milks, you bypass the transformation phase of the animal, which produces lots of methane and requires more energy to transform. The protein content of the grain or nut milk is similar to traditional animal's milk, and the missing nutrients can be added so you have comparable benefits. Take your time trying them out since they may taste different, but be sure that they have real benefits too.

Beware of big portions

Go for single portion sized plates. If you are lured in by big bargains, make sure you assess your family's capacity to consume that amount of food, so that it does not go to waste.

Take your own bags

When you go shopping for groceries, bring your own bags. Plastic bags end up at landfills and take forever to disappear. They also cause damage to the wildlife. In the ocean, for example, sea turtles die because they mistake these bags for jelly fish.

Shut your lid

When cooking food or just boiling water, put a lid on your pot to contain the heat. Not only will this reduce the heat loss and save fuel (if you have a gas stove), the food will cook more quickly.

Prepare a list

If you need to go shopping, prepare a list beforehand and most important, stick to that list. This will prevent making impulsive or spontaneous purchases.

Make your own baby food

What did people do in the days before packaged baby food? Yes, they made their own baby food! It is not that time consuming to do, and this way you can be sure of what you are feeding your baby. Make a few extra portions and deep freeze them in ice cube molds. Depending on your baby's age, you would only need one or two cubes for each serving.

Doggy bag

When going out to a restaurant, very frequently we do not finish all the food we've been served. The restaurant usually offers to pack the leftovers in a doggy bag. The problem with restaurant packaging is that typically it is made of Styrofoam, which is a cheap material. So, next time you visit your favorite restaurant, knowing that you are likely to bring back what you haven't eaten, why don't you bring your own plastic or glass container? At least it's re-usable.

Food waste

When you waste food, remember that there are people on this planet, who don't have any food to eat and some are actually starving to death. Cook and eat only what you need and do not waste the rest.

Meal planning

How many times have you caught your teen standing in front of an open refrigerator wondering what to eat? Try to show them this: Open the door and do a quick scan of what's inside the fridge, then shut the door. Once you know what you want, go for it! Don't prolong the agony.

Microwave

If you microwave often, make sure the inside stays clean. The cleaner it is, the less energy it will consume.

Oven management

If you are using the oven, make sure you are not opening the door frequently and letting the heat out. If you really need to monitor what is inside, use a thermometer. Make sure that your oven window is always clean. Also, if you have something really small to cook, use your mini-oven or microwave instead.

Pots and the stove

Make sure your pots are the right size for your burners. If the pot is smaller than the burner, lots of heat energy is lost.

Preheating

If you use your oven a lot, and need to preheat it, do it only for a limited time. Normal ovens should not take more than 10 minutes to reach the right temperature.

Refrigerator filling

When you return from a trip to the grocery store and need to unpack, take out everything from the bag. Most people take one item at a time and place it where it belongs—either in a cupboard or in the refrigerator. But when the refrigerator is opened so frequently, it consumes a lot of energy to keep the things inside cold, so try to avoid that.

Smaller grocery stores

If you are on vacation or are not in a familiar area and need to shop for food, pick smaller stores. They typically source their stuff from local distributors and their food offering varies seasonally. Larger food chains typically recycle the same products all the year round and therefore require lots of transportation when food is out of season.

Storage containers

Store leftovers in glass or porcelain containers. There won't be any chemical transfer from container to food.

Unfreezing meat

In our fast paced world, it's common to do last minute meal planning. That means taking out food from the freezer and thawing it on the counter or in the microwave. Using the microwave or stove obviously means using power, which we don't want. Even unfreezing on the counter requires using the surrounding heat that's generated by your house's heating system. In addition, meat is not something you want to leave at room temperature for too long as it may develop bacteria. In that case, the right thing to do is simply to transfer your frozen meat or meal from the deep freezer to the refrigerator the night before.

Buy local

Buy local produce as frequently as possible. That way, you will patronize local traders and food growers. Also, be wary of low prices, since in the food industry, low prices often come with pesticide use. You do not pay for the true cost since the field that was used will need years to regain its original quality or will need intensive care and added compost to be rich in nutrients after each harvest.

Personal Hygiene

This is an area where it's better to be safe than sorry.

Baby oil

Buy oil that's derived from renewable resources like nuts or fruit instead of petroleum, which is non-renewable.

Bubble bath

Use bubble bath sold in concentrated form. Not only will it last longer, it will also discourage transportation cost.

Conditioner

Buy a shampoo and conditioner combined. Having a separate bottle means the conditioner needs to be applied as a second step and will therefore require more water. If the same quantity of the product can do both jobs, why do you need an extra bottle? The impact on transportation will be twice as big.

Shaving gel

Use shaving gel that doesn't come as an aerosol. Although aerosols no longer contain CFC's which are bad for the ozone layer, they have been replaced with other petroleum-based products. It's still better to avoid them entirely.

Soap bars

Choose soap bars instead of liquid soap. They cost less, require less packaging and the packaging is often recyclable. You earn bonus points if your soap bar is made locally, has had to travel less distance and helps your local economy too!

Sunscreen

A lot of sunscreen makers claim their products are natural but that does not mean they do not contain any chemicals or preservatives. Look for natural ingredients such as vegetable oils or cocoa butter. Most important, sun protection is not only about sunscreen. It also entails wearing long-sleeved shirts, sunglasses with UV protection, a hat, or long pants when the occasion and weather permits. Use a parasol at the beach or during gardening. Don't fall asleep in broad sunlight. Limit children's exposure to sun to a fixed time, say, between 10AM and 3PM.

Sponges

First, avoid using natural sponges since exploiting them destroys their underwater habitat and impacts other life forms around them such as fish and micro-organisms. Second, replace your nylon sponge by loofas or a simple wash cloth. Nylon is made from petroleum.

Perfumes, deodorants and lotions have ingredients that we do not find naturally on earth. Since you can't become an overnight expert about all the brands and products out there, follow a few simple rules such as looking for natural products or a label that certifies that the product is organic. The ultimate change you can introduce is to ban these products from your life completely, except for soap, of course.

Care for Your Domestic Animals

Do your pet a favor

Have your pet spayed and neutered. Cats and dogs can multiply like crazy over their life span and there is currently an overpopulation of these domestic pets. Also, spaying and neutering helps animals live longer and eliminates the possibility of uterine, ovarian and testicular cancer and prostate disease.

Biodegradable bags

More and more people that walk their dogs are conscientious and gather their favorite pet's droppings. Cities, in fact, now have laws for this too. It is important that you use biodegradable bags so that the bag disappears over time along with the droppings. You will find these bags in pet stores and also in some green stores.

Buy good pet food

Most pet food brands are made with reconstituted animal by-products or low-grade wastes from beef and poultry industries. Look for the words chicken or beef, not just meat as the first ingredient on the box. Make sure that what you buy is guaranteed by the Association of American Feed Control Officials (AAFCO). Good pet food also contains vitamins A and C that act as preservatives in place of chemical preservatives, and finally, check if the food packaging is made of recycled material.

Cat litter

Traditional litter comes from mining and is not good for the environment. Once the mining is done, it takes years for the habitat to generate life again. Cat owners should avoid clumping clay litter at all costs. The clay sediment is permeated with carcinogenic silica dust that can coat little kitty's lungs. You now have recycled paper and wood residue as alternatives. The paper litter is made from recycled paper and the wood comes from reclaimed wood—both recommended products. Switch gradually; incorporate new litter slowly as your cat may not like the texture of this new material.

Exotic animals

Exotic animals are captured from the wild and carried long distances to reach your home. Removing these creatures from their natural habitat is not just bad for them, it's also bad also for the ecosystem they were once part of.

Green pet gear and products

When you are buying gear for your pet, buy things that are made in the green spirit. Cat trees are made with non-treated wood and recycled carpet or sustainable fibers such as hemp. There are also organic shampoos and skin care products available for these pets.

Letting your animal go

Do not let your animal go by sending it back into the wild even though the animal may have originally been born into the wild. Domesticated animals are accustomed to living without predators and having food available at no effort. Sending them back to the wild will probably guarantee their death. So if you no longer can take care of your animal, offer it to friends or send it to your local SPCA.

Make your own pet food

The best way to ensure that your pet's food is made with the right ingredients is to make it yourself. Before starting, consult a veterinarian or veterinary nutritionist to ensure the right balance of proteins and nutrients that your pet needs.

It would be good to remember that pets, however you may be attached to them, are not meant to live like humans. Their bodies, behaviors and instincts are those of wild animals; and they are adapted to outdoor conditions. Make sure you don't try to humanize them too much. It you do have the tendency to do that, ask yourself if you should not get a toy robot or a teddy bear instead. It will cost less, will require less care and be perfect to live indoors—just like you.

Holidays and Celebrations

Do not go overboard with buying candy. Kids in North America get more candy than they can eat or that is good for their health in general, and certainly on Halloween night. Candies are filled with sugar and empty calories. Some candy varieties are made in faraway countries and require lots of petroleum to make their way to your home. Instead, try to buy desserts for your kids that contain some nutrients. Try raisins covered in chocolate or yogurt, good chocolate, baked (not fried) chips or nachos. Make sure you also have some money left for a different cause such as donating to UNICEF.

If you must buy candy, buy organic, natural treats. Try Fair Trade sourced chocolates or candies made with cane sugar, fruit juices, and natural colors. Visit www.greenhalloween.org for more ideas.

Christmas trees

There has been lots of debate over the years about what is a greener option—to buy a real Christmas tree or an artificial one. To be sure, this really is an example of a Hobson's choice.

The artificial tree can be reused year after year and does not involve any tree cutting. On the other hand, even today, most artificial trees are not made with recyclable material and usually come from very far. In the case of the natural tree option, aside from the non green elements such as the smell, and the imperfectness of its shape, every year, another tree has to die. Some municipalities now have programs where you can pick up trees a few weeks after Christmas for composting. Also, because these trees are grown for the sole purpose of Christmas use, you are actually not taking away from the Earth. Consider the fact that over the duration of its growth (from six to ten years, depending on the climate of the locale and height of the tree), the tree would have contributed to the environment, hosted birds, rodents, and insects, and contributed to the ambient air quality. Lastly, these trees usually come from a local producer. Therefore, by buying a natural tree you contribute to local development. The verdict: The natural tree is the way to go!!

Christmas lights

First you need to assess how you can reduce the number of lights you put up during the holiday period. After that try to replace what you have with smaller lights or LED lights that, although more expensive, last much longer. Finally, put the lights on a timer, so you really don't need to have them light up at three o'clock in the morning!

Halloween costumes

Don't buy costumes that your children or you will wear only once or twice and then discard. Instead, see what you already have that can be modified as a costume. Be creative. Old clothes can make for a great retro costume. You can use cardboard boxes to make a robot. The possibilities are endless. Same goes for accessories. Buy those that you can reuse. Lastly, avoid soft vinyl found in mass-produced costumes.

Halloween pumpkin disposal

Instead of throwing it in the trash, cut the pumpkin into small pieces and put it in your compost pile.

You can eat your pumpkin, too. When carving your pumpkin, put the seeds aside. Wash them a little, throw on some salt and broil them in the oven until they are light brown. They can be eaten like chips and are healthier because they are not fried. To make sure you can eat the fruit of the pumpkin, use small Christmas lights instead of the traditional Halloween candle. Your pumpkin will not get all burned inside and you can then use the pulp for pies, soups or muffins.

Outdoors

Doing your own composting has several advantages. Composting takes up very limited space. The space required for organic garbage of an entire city is considerable, so that's becoming quite rare. City garbage dumps are generally overused and the sites are located in remote areas that you can't easily access. You can also cut down on the garbage disposal cost and lessen its impact on the environment.

As you know, having less garbage for each property means fewer garbage trucks,

> **Make Your Own Compost**
> You can make compost of anything that was once a living organism, such as kitchen and recycled garden waste. Paper products are also effective ingredients.
> It takes six to eight weeks to make good compost, depending on the ingredients you use. Compost is used to feed and condition the soil and for making potting mixes. Around 40% of the average dustbin contents are suitable for home composting. It helps cut down on landfill too.
> *Source:*
> *http://www.gardenorganic.org.uk/organicgardening/gh_comp.ph p*

less gas, fewer tractors to manage the dump, and so on. The bonus is a leaner municipal tax bill.

Some cities have a composting program where they pick up organic material from the houses and industrial areas and the taxpayers can later buy that compost, although the full benefits of composting aren't achieved that way. The most effective compost has the following ratio: 66% "dry" ingredients to 33% "humid" ingredients.

To start your compost pile with plenty of bacteria for decay, throw in a few shovels-full of aged manure or rich topsoil. Add some more during the process to keep it going. Also, keep a bag or barrel of dry leaves next to your compost pile to cover up kitchen scraps. This will deter critters and flies. If they persist, bury the kitchen scraps deeper inside the pile.

Lawn clippings

Managing lawn clippings is a big problem. Imagine the number of people who put their clippings in the trash bin every week! Did you know that leaving the clippings on your lawn actually feeds it? Keeping leaves on your lawn not only saves you time as you do not need to pick them up, but it also keeps the lawn healthy and green. Leaves are cut when composted and turn into nutrients for the soil, thereby decreasing the need for commercial fertilizers and compost. Did you also know that lawnmowers can now mulch the clippings so they are hardly noticeable once they are freshly cut, accelerating their absorption by the soil? Consider all the people and fuel needed to manage this. Wouldn't it be nice to see your municipal tax bill go down as a result?

Lawnmower

If you are thinking of replacing your lawnmower, make sure you consider the size of the area that needs to be cut. Then select the greener option. Your order of selection could be—first, the reel mower (no engine), then the electric (wireless or not), then the four strokes, and finally the two strokes. Also, reel mowers are simpler to maintain as you just need to re-sharpen the blades once in a while.

Shovel instead of snow blow

Instead of having your car entrance snow plowed by a tractor or by yourself, why not use the old shovel? Of course, shoveling depends on the size of your entrance, the amount of snow you get or the time you have available. For some, shoveling may not be a viable option. But then you could always try to make it a family activity and have your kids help out. Even a two- or three-year-old, you'll be glad to know, will be ready to shovel with you. Eventually, as the kids grow older, this can become one of the chores that need to be done every week. This includes lawn mowing in the summer or emptying out the dishwasher any other time. This is good exercise for everyone. So spend time with the family and develop your children's sense of responsibility at the same time.

Annual flowers

Everyone loves flowers! Annuals are useful for a splash of one-season color. But since replacing them each year is expensive, concentrate on just a few spots.

Avoid using pesticides

Pesticides are made from chemicals, and while they may be effective in what they are supposed to do, they can also be destructive to other natural elements in the sprayed areas. In fact, the alarming thing is that long-term effects of pesticides are still unknown. Instead, use natural pesticides. Some commonly used biological control agents could be ladybugs to control aphids, small worms, and other soft-bodied insects; lacewings to control aphids, scales, spider mites and other insects and eggs; trichogramma wasps to control moth and butterfly eggs; and Bacillus thuringiensis (Bt) to control larvae of moths, butterflies, mosquitoes and other pests.

Coffee grounds

You can use coffee grounds as mulch around acid-loving plants such as blueberries, azaleas and dogwoods.

Collect rainwater

One way to save on water consumption and give respite to the public system is to collect rainwater from your roof and put it into barrels. You can easily find such barrels at your local gardening store. The barrels are equipped with spigots, so you can plug in your hose and directly water your flowers, vegetables and lawn.

Cooler external walls

If one of your house's external walls is facing east, west or south, it probably gets very hot in the summer. Because the heat accumulates during the day, if you happen to touch the wall several hours after the sun sets, you can still feel the heat. This contributes to global warming. To offset this, you should try planting shrubs and trees close by. If you have limited gardening space, especially in an urban area, you can experiment with vines that climb and stick to the wall. They take up almost no room on the ground, need no maintenance, offer good shade for birds and absorb the heat, making the inside of the building cooler.

Fallen leaves

Let fallen leaves lie instead of raking them away. Let them settle into a bed of mulch that adds to the soil and creates insect-rich areas for ground-dwelling birds to forage.

Garden a Little

From saving water to making your own compost, gardening can be such a rewarding hobby, provided you are saving as much as you are making green.

For instance, raising a vegetable garden brings its own rewards. Try growing plants organically to keep the ecosystem intact. In the bargain, you will not just have clean, healthy food on your table—food that did not take fuel to transport—but you will also get to spend a good deal of time outside caring for your garden, which will also keep you in good shape.

Do not use chemical pesticides. Use natural products instead. If you want to fight pests, try to attract birds to your garden as they feast on parasites and natural predators such as ladybirds. Do you know that certain plants also repel insects? Herbs and flowers that fall into this category include basil, chives, mint, marigolds and chrysanthemums. Mix them with other plants to drive out pests.

Try age-old techniques like a mixture of *neem* oil and garlic oil sprayed on tree trunks and diseased plants and shrubs. It works like a miracle in curbing pests, bacteria and fungus. Try applying vinegar directly on the most stubborn ones. Also organic compost and mulch improve soil health and reduce the need for pesticides and fertilizers. Make your own compost with grass clippings and vegetable scraps from the kitchen (see box).

Grow your flowers from seeds. This may be a little tedious, but the difference in price is tempting. You can reap an entire bed of flowers or vegetables from one packet! And go for repeat harvests.

Grass selection

When getting your yard ready for grass seed, select the right kind for the area you live in. Most popular grass seeds require lots of maintenance. Clover is a variety that is usually low maintenance and needs little water while still remaining green.

Herbs

Try growing culinary herbs in a big terra cotta container near your kitchen door, in full sunlight, for convenient use.

Keep grass long

We like the golf course look—short grass. But that lets out a lot of humidity, therefore demanding water back to ensure it does not dry out. By keeping it longer, the humidity is better retained and unwanted seeds can't grow since it's too dark for that under the tall blades.

Organic soil

I bet you had no idea that a mere 5% increase in organic material quadruples the soil's ability to store water. This could add up to a significant amount in hot, dry landscapes.

Peaceful garden

Cover street noise. Sound pollution can be minimized through the use of water features, such as a waterfall, or a pond with a fountain jet. Wind chimes also help, as well as bird feeders that attract songbirds.

Pest repellents

Safe herbal pest repellents include garlic and hot pepper sprays that can easily be made by processing these herbs with water in a blender, straining out the pulp, and diluting heavily with water. Keep this solution handy to spray with a pump sprayer when needed.

Shade gardens

Shade gardens are low maintenance. They require less watering, grow slowly and have fewer weeds to fight. They also provide a cool place to rest during warm days.

Trees and shrubs on the property

Make sure your home or workplace has plenty of trees surrounding the building as they provide cool shade. Also, they keep the air clean, which is important in urban areas. If you live in a northern country, plant evergreens on the north side of your house to protect from winds. Also, plant trees with leaves on the southern side so that side remains shaded in the summer and allows the sun in during the winters.

Use native species

When selecting plant material for landscaping, always go for native plants. They are handy and accustomed to the climate and pests, therefore they need less human intervention to thrive, even under the most difficult of conditions.

Friendly insects

To create a haven for beneficial insects in your yard, provide water all year in any size container (avoid stagnant water which may attract mosquitoes), and shelter in it for a variety of plants, flowers, grasses, shrubs and trees, and food, such as pollen and nectar. Once beneficial insects, birds, and animals get to know a particular landscape as a place to find food all year, they will keep coming back.

Chlorine for the pool

You can now replace the chlorine in your pool with salt. The cost of doing this may be a little higher but it is efficient and the pool will be easier to maintain. The first thing that you need to do is purchase a salt generator that is appropriate to your pool size. These generators are usually installed in line with the existing plumbing. After that, all you need to do is throw salt straight into your pool and follow the instructions to get the water quality to the desired level. Your local pool store will explain the complete procedure.

After all is said and done, the biggest benefit in having a greener home is spending more time outdoors and getting closer to nature. This is not only good for the planet, but good for your health, too. More time outside means more oxygen, more exercise and better health. If all you have is a corner in your garden, a city park or even a balcony filled with plants, that too can be very relaxing.

Summing Up

If there is one thing we hope you will understand after reading this book and applying some of the ideas, it is that there is no end to what you can contribute to your environment, even in small measures. If at any time you venture to overhaul your habits drastically, there will still be endless opportunity for improvement and for making better choices in reducing your impact on this magnificent planet.

Index

A

A/C, 43
advertising, 35
Alternative Sources of Energy, 54
Animals, 104

B

baby food, 95
Baby oil, 101
Bamboo flooring, 74
Bargain, 20
bath, 101
batteries, 34, 47
Beans, 89
beer, 91
bio-degradable plates, 31
Bottled water, 59
Bubble bath, 101
bulbs, 45

C

car washes, 62
Carpets, 75
Cat litter, 105
Chlorine, 122
Christmas, 109
Christmas trees, 108
Cleaning products, 22
clothes, 33, 37
coffee, 93
Coffee, 116
Coffee machine, 91
cold water, 51
Cold water, 60
Conditioner, 101
Construction, 80
Construction materials, 73
Consuming Right, 25
Consumption, 19

containers, 99
Cooling, 82
curtains, 41
Cut down on napkin use, 23

D

dishes, 61
Dishwasher, 25, 60
Doggy bag, 96
doors, 82
Driveway, 62
dry, 52
Dry cleaning, 27
Dryer, 52
Dryer balls, 29
DVD, 30, 35

E

Earth Day, 36
Ecological logs, 26
electricity, 54
electronics, 33
Energy Star, 47
Energy-efficient, 40
Envelopes, 21
EPA certification, 29
Exotic animals, 105

F

Fair trade flowers, 28
Fish, 90
flowers, 115
Food, 87, 96

G

garage, 41
garden, 120
Garden, 118

125

Geothermal power, 56
Gift a service, 37
glass tiles, 78
Grass, 119
gray water, 63
Green renovation, 81
green restaurants, 28
Greening Your Home, 15
grocery stores, 98

H

Halloween costumes, 110
Halloween pumpkin, 110
Hang clothes, 52
Heat loss, 49
Heating, 82
Herbs, 120
Holidays, 108
houses, 86
Hygiene, 101

I

Ice pack, 48
insect, 122
Insulating, 82
insulation, 83

J

juice, 91
Just in case purchases, 20

L

Laundry, 51
Lawn clippings, 113
Lawnmower, 114
leaves, 117
Light tips, 44
Lighters, 29
lighting, 44
lights, 43, 44
local, 99
lumber, 78

M

Magazines subscription, 29
Meal, 96
meat, 90, 99
Microwave, 97
milk, 94
Minimum heat, 41
Motion activated lighting, 44
Movies, 30

N

napkin, 23

O

Office supplies, 28
organic, 87
Organic, 90, 91, 93
Outdoors, 112
oven, 49, 72
Oven, 97

P

Paint, 84, 85
Painting tip, 86
Pest, 121
pesticides, 115
pet, 104
pet food, 106
Phone book, 22
pipes, 41
Polyethylene, 78
pool, 122
Pots, 97
power strip, 49
Preface, 4
prostate disease., 104

R

rain water, 116
Rainwater, 69
Rechargeable batteries, 47

Recycle, 37
Recycled packaging, 26
Reduce heat, 42
refrigerator, 34, 48
Refrigerator, 48, 98
Refrigerator maintenance, 48
refurbished electronics, 30
Remote control, 49
renovation, 81
Right heating, 42
roof, 82

S

second life to products, 20
Sell your own electricity, 54
Shade grown coffee, 93
Shaving, 70
Shaving gel, 102
shoes, 22
Shovel, 114
showerheads, 63
shrubs, 121
snow blow, 114
Soap bars, 102
soil, 120
Solar power, 55
Solar water heater, 72
Sponges, 103
Storage containers, 99
stove, 97
summer, 43
Sunscreen, 102
Switch off the lights, 43

T

tap, 66
teeth, 60
tiles, 78
Timer, 46
Timer on lights, 44
tissues, 26
toilet, 21
Toilet paper, 26
Toilets, 68
toxic, 10
Trash bags, 31
Trees, 121
TV, 49

U

Unplug your TV, 49

V

vegetarianism, 87
Ventilators, 73

W

walls, 117
Wash, 51
washing dishes, 61
waste, 96
water heater, 45, 72
Wind power, 56
Window, 83
windows, 82
wine, 93
Wood, 79
Wood flooring, 79

Additional Resources

Environment

Behar, H. It's Not about The Coffee. New York: The Penguin Group, 2009.

Blackburn, William R. The Sustainability Handbook: The Complete Management Guide to Achieving Social, Economic, and Environmental Responsibility. London: Earthscan, 2007.

Elkington, John. Cannibals with Forks: The Triple Bottom Line of 21st Century Business. Oxford: Capstone Publishing, 1997.

Esty, Daniel C., & Winston, Andrew S. Green to Gold. N-J: John Wiley & Sons, 2006.

Friedman, Frank B. Practical Guide to Environmental Management. 10th ed.

Washington, D.C. Environmental Law Institute, 2006.

Gordon, P.J. Lean and Green. San Francisco: Berrett-Koehler Publishers Inc, 2001.

Hawken, P., Lovins, A., Lovins, L. Natural Capitalism. New York: Back Bay Books, 1999.

Hawken, P. The Ecology of Commerce. New York: Harper Collins Publishers, 1993.

Holliday, Charles O., Jr., Stephan Schmidheiny, and Philip Watts. Walking the Talk: The Business Case for Sustainable Development. Sheffield, UK: Greenleaf Publishing, 2002.

Lockwood, Charles. Harvard Business Review on Green Business Strategy. Boston: Harvard Business School Publishing Corporation, 2007.

Lourie, B., Smith, R. Slow Death by Rubber Duck. Canada: Alfred A. Knopf, 2009.

Malower, J. Strategies for the Green Economy. McGraw Hill, 2009.

McDilda, D.G. 365 Ways to Live Green. Avon: Adams Media, 2008.

Mintzer, Rich. Green Business. Entrepreneur Media Inc, 2009.

Petrini, Carlo. Slow Food Nation: Why Our Food Should Be Good, Clean, and Fair. New York: Rizzoli Ex Libris, 2005.

Prakash, Aseem. Greening the Firm. Cambridge, UK: Cambridge University Press, 2000.

Robèrt, K-H. The Natural Step Story, Seeding a Quiet Rrevolution. United States: New Catalyst Books, 2002.

Rogers, E., Kostigen,T. The Green Book. New York: Crown Publishing Group, 2007.

Savitz, Andrew. The Triple Bottom Line: How Today's Best-Run Companies Are Achieving Economic, Social, and Environmental Success-and How You Can Too. Hoboken, N-J: John Wiley & Sons, 2006.

Suzuki, D. The Sacred Balance: Rediscovering Our Place in Nature. Vancouver: Greystone Books, 2002.

Suzuki, D., Boyd, D.R. David Suzuki's Green Guide. Greystone Books, 2008.

Vasil, A. Ecoholic: Your Guide to the Most Environmentally-Friendly Information, Products and Services in Canada. Canada: Random House, 2007.

Wallace, T., Bonin, J., McKay, K. True Green @ Work. National Geographic Society, 2008.

Motivation, inspiration

If you agree with the ideas in this book but think you have good reasons for not undertaking to do things differently, read the books below. They'll provide you with the motivation you need!

Babauta, L. The Power of Less. New York: Hyperion, 2009.

Ferris, T. The 4-hour Work Week. New York: Crown Publishers, 2007.

Schwartz, David J. The Magic of Thinking Big. New York: Fireside, 2007.

Web-Based Resources

www.naturalstep.org This organization has helped big corporations with their framework and concepts; they can also help you make better decisions.

www.Ecogeek.org Small site frequently updated with articles on green topics and tips on how people can make a difference.

www.greenblue.org This website focuses on sustainable product design and organizational practices.

www.treehugger.com TreeHugger is the leading media outlet dedicated to driving sustainability mainstream.

www.eatwellguide.org The Eat Well Guide® is a free online directory for anyone in search of fresh, locally grown, and sustainably-produced food in the United States and Canada.

www.slowfood.com The official slow food website.

www.davidsuzuki.org The David Suzuki Foundation has worked to find ways for society to live in balance with the natural world. The Foundation uses science and education to promote solutions that conserve nature and help achieve sustainability.

Environmental footprint calculators

Here are several sites to calculate your environmental footprint. Each one is different, and each has pros and cons. The bottom line is that what you choose to do is a matter of personal preference. Look at how each tool is built and the information it collects. Notice also that each is also a matter of precision: some are very general, and in those cases it is hard to see the impact of the changes we make.

From the environmental protection agency (EPA):

http://www.epa.gov/climatechange/emissions/ind_calculator.html

and some others:

http://www1.wattzon.com/?redirected-from-old=1

http://coolclimate.berkeley.edu/uscalc

http://www.nature.org/initiatives/climatechange/calculator/

http://www.carbonfootprint.com/calculator.aspx

http://www.safeclimate.net/calculator/

And here is one intended for kids:

http://calc.zerofootprint.net/youth/

www.ingramcontent.com/pod-product-compliance
Lightning Source LLC
Chambersburg PA
CBHW051653040426
42446CB00009B/1121